Exploring the Cornish Coast

David Chapman

Alison Hodge

First published in 2008 by
Alison Hodge, 2 Clarence Place, Penzance,
Cornwall TR18 2QA, UK
www.alisonhodgepublishers.co.uk
info@alison-hodge.co.uk

Reprinted 2011

ISBN-13 978-0-906720-56-1

British Library Cataloguing-in-Publication Data
A catalogue record for this book is available from
the British Library.

Designed and originated by BDP –
Book Development & Production, Penzance,
Cornwall

Printed in China

Key
(CH) = Cliff and Heath
(ES) = Estuary and Creek
(RP) = Rock Pools
(SD) = Sand Dunes

Title page: Shingle beach at Loe Bar, near Porthleven

Contents

Introduction

Duckpool, near Coombe Valley, North Cornwall

The coastline is Cornwall's greatest asset. Not only is it impressive and beautiful, it also has great variety. From sheltered coves to long, sandy beaches, to storm-blasted head-lands, Cornwall's coast has it all. Around the coast this variety of habitat has wide appeal to wildlife: it is the county's single most important unbroken nature reserve, and we all have access to the whole of it.

Whatever your reason for making use of the Cornish coastline, it would be difficult to remain unmoved by the nature which can be seen there. Highlights of the year include the stunning flowers of spring when the coastal strip is splashed liberally with the colours of thrift, trefoil, vetch and squill. In late spring we have the annual migration of the basking sharks, which tempt us with glimpses of their dorsal fins and tails. Summer brings even more flowers, and a huge variety of insects, such as the dark green fritillaries and silver-studded blues of the dune systems. The coastal heaths burst into colour with heather, bell heather and western gorse in August and September. In autumn we witness a steady movement of birds passing south and west, with waders very much a feature of the estu-aries and creeks. Late autumn usually brings a storm or two, and then a bit of beach combing to search for goose barnacles is the order of the day. Winter isn't dull either, since this is when our estuaries bulge under the weight of waders and wildfowl. Throughout the year we have the chance of seeing the world's most exciting cetacean, the bottle-nose dolphin; the world's fastest bird of prey, the peregrine and, of course, England's only breeding red-billed crows, the choughs! All of this, from the Cornish coastline.

David Chapman, 2008

About this Book

This book aims to introduce the nature of the Cornish coastline, from how it was originally formed to what lives there now. I shall break down the coast into four distinct habitats, which progress from the inter-tidal region up the beaches and on to the dry land around the coast path. These habitats are: Rock Pools; Beaches and Sand Dunes; Estuary and Creek, and Cliff and Heath. Within each section I shall pick out the species which I feel are most typical of that habitat. I shall try to show all of the common species as well as some of the less common but interesting Cornish specialities. Within each section, the species are ordered in a consistent manner, beginning with mammals, followed by birds, reptiles, amphibians, insects and flowers. There is, of course, cross-over between these habitats, so although stonechat, for example, is listed under 'Cliff and Heath', because that is the habitat with which this bird is most often associated, it can also be seen in dunes, so I use a cross-referencing system to indicate this fact: (CH) = Cliff and Heath; (ES) = Estuary and Creek; (RP) = Rock Pools, and (SD) = Sand Dunes.

When choosing the species to include in this book I started by picking those whose distribution in Cornwall is predominantly coastal, but I have also looked for species that are found commonly on the coast, or which in one way or another typify the coast. It is inevitable that species not listed here will occur along the coast; such examples will include rarer species, and those that are less typical of the coast. For each species (with the exception of the strandline and some of the rock pool), a calendar of months illustrates when the species can be seen. For flowers, these calendars refer to when the plant is in flower; for animals the calendars show when they are not hibernating; for birds the calendars show when they are present in the county, and for insects they show when the adult form is present.

My aim is to use non-specialist language throughout the book, but where there is no alternative I shall explain any specialist words at the point of use. At the back of the book is a gazetteer of places good for coastal wildlife, which can be used to plan a visit to a coastal location.

Rock Pools (RP)

One of the happiest memories I have of childhood holidays is of rock-pooling, and whenever I am visited by my niece and nephews they too love to explore the pools around our coast. It is only relatively recently that I have learnt that you don't have to be a child to enjoy this fascinating hobby: to delve into a rock pool is to take a peep into a completely different world – one that contains creatures with adaptations which seem alien to us.

The formation of rock pools is fairly straightforward. They are associated with rocky coasts, and are formed when the sea cuts into a cliff, creating a flat, rocky area beneath the cliff – an area known appropriately as a 'wave-cut platform'. Some of the most interestingly shaped wave-cut platforms occur on the north coast of Cornwall, where the rock strata have previously been twisted and now slope at a steep angle to the horizontal. Here the ocean has created a beach with long, thin rock pools interspersed with ridges of rock.

My local beach for rock-pooling is at Godrevy, which is extremely well situated for a diverse range of wildlife-watching. Here we have the nearby dunes – a great location for sea-watching, with potential for dolphins and seals, and a convenient area of rocks exposed at low tide.

Probably the most well used rock pools in the county are at Polzeath, where there is a Voluntary Marine Conservation Area and a visitor centre aimed at encouraging us all to appreciate and protect the marine environment. The Voluntary Marine Conservation Area, established in July 1995, stretches from Daymer Bay to Pentire Point – a length of around three miles. The visitor centre is open during the summer, when a warden is employed to provide information to people and to take groups out rock-pooling. The rock-pooling trips are free of charge, and offer an excellent way to learn more about the creatures found in this environment. The centre is owned and financed by North Cornwall District Council, to whom we should give our support for this excellent venture.

Obviously rock-pooling is best at low tide, when the greatest areas of rocks are revealed by the retreating sea. It is safest to start rock-pooling a couple of hours before low tide, so

you crossed to get to the rocks, and which now form an island. It is best not to go rock-pooling alone, and always be cautious.

The creatures that get trapped in rock pools by the retreating tide are usually very hardy and adaptable. They face an uncertain time while the tide is out. The pools in which they sit can warm up considerably in the heat of the sun, which can also cause evaporation and increased salinity. During heavy rain, the water in these pools can become less saline, but crabs, anemones, fish and crustacea all manage to survive until the next inundation by the sea. However, if we catch creatures and take them out of that environment it is our responsibility to return them safely. It might not seem important to us that creatures should be replaced where they were caught, but consider the Cornish sucker fish that has just laid eggs under a particular stone. That fish does not just leave those eggs: it will stay and defend them against predation. If we move it to another rock pool, then we risk the eggs being lost and causing distress to the creature involved.

There are a number of points we should all adhere to when delving into rock pools. These address our own safety as well as the well-being of wildlife.

that you can follow the tide out. As soon as the tide turns extra caution must be taken, since it is then possible to be cut off by the sea. It isn't beyond the realms of possibility that you become so engrossed by the activity that you forget about that last gulley

The Seashore Code

- Do not take live specimens from the beach, always leave live animals where you find them.
- If you look under rocks always replace them, carefully, where they were.
- Do not remove seaweed from rocks.
- Only take shells home if you are sure they are empty.
- Many seashells that are for sale in shops had animals living inside them when they were collected; examine your conscience before buying them.
- Do not leave litter on the beaches.
- Please report any unusual wildlife that is stranded on the beach.
- Before venturing on to the rocks, always check the tide times, and keep one eye on the sea.
- When fishing take care not to leave behind old nets, hooks and lines.

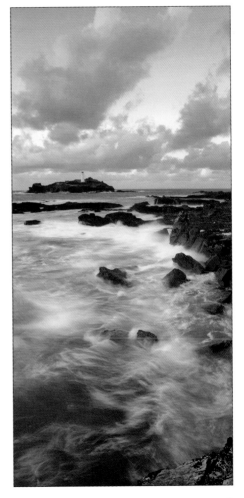

Godrevy Point is one of the best places on the coast for wildlife watching, and that includes a good selection of rock pools

Rock Pool Species

Purple Sandpiper
Calidris maritima

The purple sandpiper is a rather dumpy wader with short legs and a sooty brown plumage, slightly paler underneath. Orange legs and base of bill. This is a bird found exclusively on rocky beaches during winter. Habitually returns to the same locations each year. Good spots include the rocks near the Jubilee Pool in Penzance.

Turnstone
Arenaria interpres

One of our most familiar waders because it frequents harbours as well as rocky beaches. Can be extremely approachable as it runs around turning stones and seaweed in search of food. Plumage may be a bit of a mish mash of brown, white and ginger tones, depending upon age and time of year, but always shows a dark bib and flashes of white in the wings when in flight. Photo: winter plumage. (ES)

| J | F | M | A | M | J | J | A | S | O | N | D |

| J | F | M | A | M | J | J | A | S | O | N | D |

Five-bearded Rockling

Ciliata mustela

Rocklings are a little eel-like in shape, though not quite as long, growing up to 20 cm. The five-bearded rockling has two barbels above the upper lip, two on the upper lip and one on the chin. There is also a three-bearded form. Rocklings are found in rock pools around the county.

Common Blenny
Blennius pholis

The common blenny is the commonest fish of rock pools. Also known as the shanny. May reach 16 cm long. Colour is brown, though male becomes darker when breeding.

Montagu's Blenny
Blennius montagui

This species has a uniquely shaped crest, with a row of small tentacles between the crest and the dorsal fin. Overall colour is olive brown, but has bluish-grey spots and darker vertical bands on its flanks. Quite a small blenny, only growing up to 8 cm long. Within Britain this species is found only in the South West.

Tompot Blenny
Blennius gattorugine

A very large blenny, the tompot sometimes grows to 30 cm long. This species has a much-branched, ornate tentacle above each eye. Olive brown with dark vertical stripes which cross the dorsal fin, tail and flanks. Face is mottled. Was named because it is often caught in crab pots.

Cornish Sucker Fish
Lepadogaster lepadogaster

The Cornish sucker fish is also known as the shore clingfish. This species is flattened in shape to allow it to get under rocks. Underneath its head it has a sucker disc which enables it to hold tight to rocks. From above, the most distinctive feature is the two blue spots behind the eyes. Its eyes are quite large, its dorsal fin merges with its tail, and it has flattened, duck-billed shaped mouth parts. Its golden eggs, laid under stones, are guarded by one or both parents. Grows up to 8 cm long.

Edible Crab
Cancer pagurus
Probably the most distinctive feature of the edible crab is its pasty-shaped carapace, showing the distinctive crimped edge. Its colour is almost brick red. Can grow to over 25 cm across. Found in crevices between rocks at low tide.

Shore Crab
Carcinus maenas
Sometimes called the 'green shore crab', this species is usually olive green, but is patterned with various other shades of brown and even white. This is the most commonly encountered crab of rock pools. It is a much smaller species than the edible crab, most specimens being less than 10 cm across. The front edge of its carapace is sharp and toothed.

Broad-clawed Porcelain Crab
Porcellana platycheles

This is a tiny species of crab found in small crevices and under stones in rock pools. Its round carapace reaches only 2 cm across, but its two pincers are huge, in relation to the body size, and flattened. Its body and legs are fringed with coarse hairs, making this a very well camouflaged species, often difficult to distinguish its shape.

Spider Crab
Maja squinado

A huge species of crab, its carapace grows up to 20 cm long, and its pincers up to 45 cm long. Has a very pointed carapace, longer than it is wide, which is not as flattened as the other species of crab listed here. Colour is brick red. This is found in deeper rock pools and crevices among rocks.

Velvet Swimming Crab

Macropipus puber

The velvet swimming crab is a very dark crab with distinctive red eyes. This is an aggressive species, so be careful if handling it. Its carapace is velvety and flattened as are its legs, which are used for swimming. The legs are also fringed by coarse hairs to assist in propulsion. Grows up to about 7 cm. Found fairly commonly in rock pools and in cracks.

Hermit Crab

Eupagurus bernhardus

Hermit crabs utilize the shells of molluscs in which to live. The commonest of the hermit crabs in Cornwall is often referred to as the 'common hermit crab', and it is also the largest.

Common Prawn
Leander serratus
Commonly found trapped in rock pools at low tide. The common prawn has a semi-translucent body with spots and lines. It has very long antennae, and a long, saw-like rostrum (extension of head in front of eyes). It grows up to about 6 cm long.

Common Shrimp
Clangon vulgaris
The common shrimp is more often associated with sandy areas, but can be found in rock pools. It is smaller than the common prawn, growing up to a maximum of 5 cm. Lacks the prawn's long rostrum. Semi-translucent with a pinkish flush and spots.

Sea Slater
Ligia oceanica
Essentially resembling a woodlouse, the sea slater is found among the rocks and seaweed of the seashore. Particularly active at dusk. Brown in colour, with a segmented body which grows up to 3 cm long.

Beadlet Anemone
Actinia equina
Probably the commonest anemone in Cornwall, the beadlet anemone is found in most rock pools. Opens when immersed in water; closes to conserve moisture when exposed. Most commonly red/brown, but can be greenish in colour. Has a ring of violet-blue 'beads' around its tentacles. Grows to a height of about 5 cm.

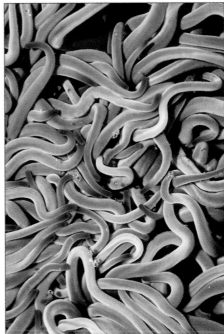

Strawberry Anemone
Actinia fragacea
The strawberry anemone is similar to a beadlet anemone, but with a distinctive patterning of yellow dots making it resemble a strawberry. It can grow to a height of 10 cm.

Snakelocks Anemone
Anemonia sulcata
This species cannot withdraw its tentacles completely, so its distinctive mass of flowing tentacles can be seen all the time. The green tentacles are usually tipped with purple, making a beautiful combination of colours.

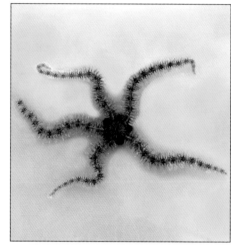

Cushion Star

Asterina gibbosa

A small starfish growing up to just 5 cm across. Its colour is variable and can be green or brown. Interestingly, it begins life as a male and changes to female at the age of four years. The cushion star is relatively common, but difficult to find.

Common Brittlestar

Ophiothrix fragilis

The common brittlestar is a relatively large brittlestar, whose central disc can grow to be 1½ cm across. Its arms are very spiny. Usually pale purplish-brown with bands across the arms. Commonly found among seaweed in rock pools.

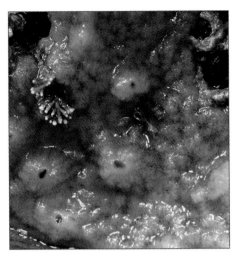 

Breadcrumb Sponge
Halichondria panicea

The most commonly occurring sponge on our rocky shores, look for the breadcrumb sponge when the tide is at its lowest. Colour can be green or, more commonly, orange. Looks like the surface of the moon, with craters through which it filters sea water to find food.

Star Ascidian
Botryllus schlosseri

Like the breadcrumb sponge, the star ascidian is an animal which encrusts itself on rocks. In appearance it is a series of creamy-white flower shapes, or stars, set against a body of purplish-brown.

Common Limpet

Patella vulgata

The limpet has a thick, conical shell, which is deeply ridged. Underneath, the limpet has a large sucker with which it attaches itself to a rock. Each limpet has its own home-scar to which it returns after feeding on algae. A limpet can live for up to 16 years and reach a size of 6 cm.

Southern Barnacle

Chthamalus stellatus

Several types of barnacle occur in Cornwall. They grow up to 1½ cm across, and typically have six wall plates which are usually heavily ridged. Their aperture is approximately oval in shape.

Common Mussel

Mytilus edulis

The common mussel is a familiar bivalve with purple or blue-grey shell. Inside, the shell is coated with mother of pearl. The shell can grow up to 9 cm wide. The common muscle attaches to rocks using tough threads.

Dog Whelk
Nucella lapillus

The dog whelk has a thick, conically shaped spiral shell which can grow to as much as 4 cm long. Colour varies enormously: most common specimens are brown or cream, but some are banded including orange. Yellow eggs are shaped like skittles and are found in ranks attached to rocks. Dog whelks prey on mussels by drilling a hole through their shell before ingesting the contents. Common on rocky shores. Photo: dog whelk with eggs.

Top Shell
Gibbula umbilicalis

There are many species of top shells. Many have brightly coloured shells with only a few whorls, giving a compact appearance. Inside the shell is a mother of pearl lining.

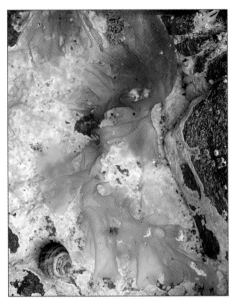

Sea Lettuce
Ulva lactuca

The sea lettuce is a green, membranous seaweed which is common in rock pools. Its shape can be difficult to determine because it can become detached and broken by the sea. Length up to 30 cm.

Gutweed
Enteromorpha intestinalis

A green, membranous seaweed, gutweed grows in a tubular fashion and, when in water, resembles a gut. When left high and dry this seaweed simply smothers the rocks to which it is fastened. It is often found in good quantities where fresh water flows over a beach. Grows up to 1 m in length.

Toothed Wrack (Saw Wrack)

Fucus serratus

The fronds of the toothed wrack are olive-brown and flat, their edges serrated like a saw. It has a midrib but no gas bladders. Found on the lower shore, and grows up to 60 cm long.

Bladder Wrack

Fucus vesiculosus

The bladder wrack has dark olive or brown fronds which have a midrib. Has swollen reproductive bodies at the tips of the fronds which are in forked pairs. Also has gas bladders occurring in pairs along its length. Grows up to 1 m long, but usually much shorter.

Egg Wrack

Ascophyllum nodosum

This species typically grows to around a metre in length, but can be even longer. It is yellow to olive-green in colour and has gas bladders regularly spaced along its length. Also known as knotted wrack, egg wrack grows on the upper and mid shore. It often plays host to a red alga, *Polysiphonia lanosa*.

Channelled Wrack

Pelvetia canaliculata

This species is found at the higher end of the inter-tidal zone. It is quite small, at up to 15 cm long, and olive-green in colour. It doesn't have gas bladders, but has swollen reproductive bodies at the tips of its fronds. Its main characteristic feature is the way in which its fronds fold over to create a gutter or channel shape.

Japweed
Sargassum muticum

An olive-brown species, Japweed has fronds growing up to 1 m in length, and small gas bladders. A species introduced with commercial oysters, which is quite common in Cornwall and becoming more so.

Sea Belt
Laminaria saccharina

A very distinctive species which can grow to 4 m long. Its olive-green or brownish blade is ribbon-shaped with crinkled edges. When hung out to dry it soon becomes soft and limp in humid conditions, so was once used as a predictor of weather, and is sometimes known as the 'poor man's weather glass'.

Kelp
Laminaria digitata
Kelp is a dark, olive-brown seaweed forming robust, flexible straps which are attached by a strong 'holdfast' to rocks. Can grow to about 1 m in length. Often forms dense stands on the lower shore. Also known as tangleweed and oarweed.

Mermaid's Tresses
Chorda filum
A long, thin, slimy, cord-like seaweed filled with gas, mermaid's tresses grows to about 6 m long and 5 mm wide. It is olive-brown in colour.

Purple Laver
Porphyra umbilicalis
A thin, membranous seaweed, purple laver looks shapeless when left high and dry by the tide. Varies in colour from green to purplish-brown, and grows up to 20 cm across.

Coralina Weed
Coralina officinalis
Common in rock pools, this species has an attractive, fan-shaped form. Its pinkish-purple fronds have white tips. Coralina weed grows up to 12 cm tall.

Coraline Crust
Lithophyllum incrustans
A calcareous alga growing on rocks, usually on those areas which remain submerged in rock pools at low tide. It is pinkish in colour and grows to a thickness of up to 2 cm, though thin coatings are commoner.

Beaches and Sand Dunes (SD)

Apart from rocks and mud (which are covered in separate chapters), the other substrates found around the coast of Cornwall are sand and shingle. These are included in one chapter because many of the plant species which have adapted to life in one can also be found in the other. Both offer difficult conditions in which to grow, with little compost and a constantly moving medium. Probably the most challenging factor is the lack of water, and that is why the species most heavily adapted to life here have such huge root systems. Marram grass, for example, has roots which form a complete entangled network under the surface of dunes. This benefits the grass, and also stabilizes the dunes.

Sea holly, which can be found growing in sand dunes and shingle, has thorny leaves with a thick cuticle, which are intended to prevent the leaves being grazed and to cut down on water loss. Possibly less obvious is the reason for the colour of their leaves. Although they contain chlorophyll, the dominant colour of a sea holly's leaf is a silvery grey – a colour which reflects more light and heat, thus protecting the plant from over-heating.

Another adaptation which the sea holly has developed is an incredibly deep root system, growing down to a depth of two metres to find fresh water.

In the dunes, rabbits are omnipresent. Here they find ideal conditions, including easy ground to dig and plenty of grass to eat. They get most of their water from plants, but some plants are reluctant to give up their hard-found moisture too easily. The sea spurge, for example, has succulent leaves which might be an obvious target for a thirsty rabbit, but for the fact that the water is stored as a bitter-tasting white sap.

Rabbits play an important part in keeping the grass short, so encouraging a diverse range of flowers in the more stable areas of dunes. Species such as bird's-foot trefoil are vital for many of the species of insect that live here. The silver-studded blue butterfly is one species that lays its eggs on the leaves of the bird's-foot trefoil. If the grass were allowed to get too long then many of the flowers would be overwhelmed, but a couple of species of

Right: Marram grass grows on the sand dunes of Constantine Bay

flower have evolved to tackle the problem head on. Yellow rattle and eyebright are both semi-parasitic plants, taking nutrients and water direct from the roots of the surrounding grasses, thus helping themselves and causing a much slower growth in the grass.

The dunes of Cornwall are not without water. Our two most extensive systems, near Hayle and Penhale, both have dune slacks, which are areas of water standing in dips within the dunes. Penhale dunes, which are the tallest in England, have quite extensive pools, and even a river during wet periods, all of which stand on a layer of clay underneath the sand. These areas of water attract amphibians and even grass snakes, but also offer a lifeline to the many birds that live here. One of the most obvious species of bird in the dunes is the skylark, which can usually be heard singing while hovering high overhead.

Even with marram grass dominating on the sandier parts, dunes are a constantly changing environment. Winds blow up sand from the beach which is carried only as far as a sheltered spot, usually in the lee of a hummock, hill or dune. The exposed face of a dune is subject to sand being removed by strong winds; the sheltered slope has sand deposited, and thus the hill moves away from the sea, only to be replaced by another in front

of it. The movement of the dunes decreases the further inland the dune is situated, so it is here that we see a greater diversity of plant life. In turn we get a greater build-up of decaying vegetative matter, and therefore the scope for non-specialist species increases.

To conserve the natural flora and fauna of the dune systems, conservationists tackle encroaching scrub such as gorse, sea buckthorn and blackthorn, using brush cutters and grazing animals. To this end, in recent years we have seen Shetland ponies grazing on Gwithian Towans and Penhale dunes.

Shingle beaches present similar problems for plants because they too contain little vegetative matter and are constantly on the move, but their formation is usually due to climate change and sea-level rise. A classic example is the beach at the mouth of the River Cober, known as Loe Bar. This bar is technically a 'barrier beach', because it completely blocks off the river from the sea.

Before the last Ice Age, the River Cober would have flowed straight out to sea. Since then the melting ice has created an enormous rise in sea level. The encroaching edge of the sea gradually gathered shingle from locations which are now submerged far from land, and pushed it up against the cliffs. At Loe Bar the sea would have had a bit of a fight with the

Gwithian Beach

river, since the river would have constantly tried to open up a path through the shingle, but here the river is small and the force of the ocean strong, so there was really no competition.

Also listed in this chapter are some of the many and varied creatures that are occasionally washed up on our shoreline. The most productive beachcombing is carried out on sandy beaches during or after autumnal storms. Goose barnacles, for example, are a regular occurrence in such conditions. These creatures attach themselves to floating debris and are at the mercy of the ocean currents. Another creature regularly washed up during the autumn, and sometimes in vast numbers, is called the 'by-the-wind-sailor'; there have been times in recent years when the whole strandline around much of the county has been smothered in the decaying bodies of these creatures – a sad but awe-inspiring sight. Whatever the season, it is always interesting to look along the strandline of a beach, particularly when you consider that the currents which bring sea water to the coast of Cornwall come from the Gulf of America.

Beach and Sand Dune Species

Field Vole
Microtus agrestis
A very common small mammal of dunes and long grass. Has a short tail and small eyes. Its fur covers its entire body, including its ears, which makes them indistinguishable. Look for its runs and nests among the base of tall grasses and wildflowers. Is the main prey of the kestrel, among other predators. (CH)

Rabbit
Oryctolagus cunniculus
Rabbits can be extremely numerous on sand dunes, where they can feed on grass and easily make burrows in the sand. As well as their burrows, also look for the many small scrapes made by rabbits at the edges of their territories. (CH, ES)

J F M A M J J A S O N D

J F M A M J J A S O N D

Sanderling
Calidris alba

This is the small white and grey wader which runs around like a clockwork toy at the edge of the waves on sandy beaches. Its legs move incredibly quickly, to keep the bird in touch with the breaking waves where it finds its food. Has a black bill and legs and a beady black eye. Plumage can look browner in late summer, when it may show the remnants of a breast band. Juveniles show some dark plumage in their wings, which forms a dark shoulder patch. Photo: winter plumage. (ES)

| J | F | M | A | M | J | J | A | S | O | N | D |

Ringed Plover
Charadrius hiaticula

The ringed plover is a small wader which breeds on sandy or shingle beaches, but is now restricted to the Isles of Scilly as a breeding bird. Outside the breeding season it can be found on beaches (both sand and shingle) and estuaries around the county. Its plumage is basically brown above and white below, but it has black rings around its neck and head. The legs and bill are orange though the bill has a black tip. Has less colour in winter. Photo: summer plumage. (CH, ES)

| J | F | M | A | M | J | J | A | S | O | N | D |

Skylark
Alauda arvensis

The skylark is a common breeding bird on sand dunes and rough grassland along the coast. Looks a little like a small thrush with a crest, but is made obvious through its song. The song is most commonly uttered while hovering high in the sky, when the skylark is an easy bird to identify but often difficult to find. (CH)

Grass Snake
Natrix natrix

Grass snakes are never numerous in Cornwall, but live in damp, grassy areas. Dune slacks provide ideal habitat for them, and the dunes of Penhale are a good location for them. The grass snake is much larger than the adder, but is harmless to us.

| J | F | M | A | M | J | J | A | S | O | N | D |

| J | F | M | A | M | J | J | A | S | O | N | D |

Palmate Newt
Triturus helvetica
The only species of newt in Cornwall is the palmate newt. This species will make a home in any area of fresh water, and is common in dune slacks. Newts return to the water to breed and lay eggs, but for most of the year they live a terrestrial lifestyle, hiding from the heat of the sun underneath logs and rotting vegetation. (CH)

Common Frog
Rana temporaria
The common frog can be found in areas of fresh water, including dune slacks. Emerging from hibernation in February they lay spawn which can be seen developing into tadpoles throughout the spring. Frogs can be distinguished from toads by their smoother skin and often thinner appearance; they are more inclined to hop, while toads walk. (CH)

| J | F | M | A | M | J | J | A | S | O | N | D |

| J | F | M | A | M | J | J | A | S | O | N | D |

Common Toad
Bufo bufo
Common toads can be found in dune slacks. Male toads are smaller than females. The toad has a warty skin when compared with a frog. Their lifestyle is similar to that of a frog. Photo: male on top of female. (CH)

Silver-studded Blue
Plebejus argus
The silver-studded blue is a tiny butterfly. The male is deep blue on his upperwings with a white fringe. Females are a dull, sooty brown. The underwings are brown or grey with black spots in the centre and a fringe of orange spots containing silvery-blue 'studs'. Frequently uses bird's-foot trefoil or heather as foodplants for its caterpillars. Flies during sunny periods, and rests when the sun disappears behind a cloud. Photo: female above male. (CH)

Dark Green Fritillary
Mesoacidalia aglaia
The dark green fritillary is a medium-to-large butterfly. Orange upperwings with dark spots make an attractive and striking patterning. The underside of the hindwing is green with large, silver-white spots. Found on sand dunes using violets as a foodplant for its caterpillars.

Cinnabar Moth
Tyria jacobeae
A medium-sized moth, largely nocturnal but can be seen flying by day, particularly if disturbed. Forewing is black with a red margin, hindwing is red. Larvae, which are orange and black, feed on ragwort and take on some of its poison, making it poisonous itself. (CH)

J	F	M	A	M	J	J	A	S	O	N	D

J	F	M	A	M	J	J	A	S	O	N	D

Sea Buckthorn

Hippophae rhamnoides

A dense shrub growing almost exclusively on dunes. Its leaves are narrow and silvery, resembling those of a willow tree. Its flowers are fairly insignificant, but the berries which grow only on the female bushes are a striking orange colour, though they soon fade in the autumn. Grows up to about 5 m high.

Yellow Horned Poppy

Glaucium flavum

A large, flamboyant plant found almost exclusively on shingle and sand. The large yellow flowers are between 6 and 8 cm across and have thin, paper-like petals. The seed pods grow occasionally to 30 cm long and are the 'horns' in the species name. The stem and leaf colour is bluish-green.

| J | F | M | A | M | J | J | A | S | O | N | D |

| J | F | M | A | M | J | J | A | S | O | N | D |

Sea Rocket

Cakile maritima

An attractive flower often found growing through the sand at the back of beaches and on dunes. Grows up to between 15 and 60 cm tall. Has pale pink flowers which have four petals and are borne in a loose spike. The leaves are fleshy.

Wild Mignonette

Reseda lutea

A large plant often forming clumps with tall (up to 80 cm) flower stems. The small, pale yellow flowers are born in spikes all around the central stem, and one plant will have many spikes. Its leaves are divided into pairs of long, narrow lobes. Grows on sand dunes.

J	F	M	A	M	J	J	A	S	O	N	D

J	F	M	A	M	J	J	A	S	O	N	D

Biting Stonecrop
Sedum acre

A small succulent plant (5 to 10 cm tall) which grows low and in clumps. Its small yellow flowers (1 cm across) have five thin petals and are borne at the top of each stem. The leaves are tiny and fleshy. Grows commonly on sand dunes, also rocks and shingle. (CH)

J	F	M	A	M	J	J	A	S	O	N	D

Bird's-foot Trefoil
Lotus corniculatus

A prostrate plant rarely growing very tall, found commonly around the coast of the county. Its yellow flowers often contain orange or red and are up to 2 cm long. Its leaves are compound with five oval leaflets. Its seed head often resembles a bird's foot. (CH, ES)

J	F	M	A	M	J	J	A	S	O	N	D

Common Storksbill

Erodium cicutarium

A tiny, prostrate plant growing among the grasses, largely on sand dunes, with small, pink or white five-petalled flowers. The leaves are fern-like, but softly hairy. The seed heads were likened to storks' bills, and explode in a twisting fashion to release the seeds.

| J | F | M | A | M | J | J | A | S | O | N | D |

Sea Spurge

Euphorbia paralias

A distinctive plant which grows in clumps on beaches and dunes. Its leaves are fleshy grey-green and grow around the tall stem (up to 70 cm), dying from the bottom first. Flowers are fairly insignificant. When the stem is broken a white sap oozes out.

| J | F | M | A | M | J | J | A | S | O | N | D |

Evening Primrose
Oenothera biennis

An erect plant growing up to 1½ m tall on waste ground and dunes. The large, pale yellow flowers have four flimsy petals which span about 5 cm and grow around the tall central stem. The leaves also grow around the stem, and are short-stalked and spear-shaped. This is a seventeenth-century introduction from North America.

Sea Holly
Eryngium maritimum

An aptly named plant, the sea holly grows on dunes and shingle. The small blue flowers grow in a spherical-shaped head which can be about 3 cm across. The silvery-green leaves have very sharp spines.

| J | F | M | A | M | J | J | A | S | O | N | D |

| J | F | M | A | M | J | J | A | S | O | N | D |

Cowslip
Primula veris

A distinctive flower growing on sandy soils particularly around the north coast of Cornwall. The straight, stout stems grow to a height of about 10 cm tall and are topped by a cluster of yellow flowers, each in a pale green calyx. The leaves are like a primrose and form a basal rosette. The best places in the county are probably Polly Joke and Penhale.

Sea Bindweed
Calystegia soldanella

A creeping plant which grows on sandy soils, particularly sand dunes. The large (5-cm diameter) flowers are funnel-shaped, and coloured white and pink in stripes emanating from the centre. The leaves are heart-shaped. The stems have no strength, and though the plant occasionally climbs it usually just sprawls.

Lady's Bedstraw
Galium verum

A sprawling plant rarely growing to any great height, but often up to 80 cm long. Its small, yellow flowers have four tiny petals and are borne in soft-looking spikes. The tiny, narrow leaves grow in whorls around the stem. Has a sweet scent which is probably why this was often used to stuff mattresses.

J	F	M	A	M	J	J	A	S	O	N	D

Viper's Bugloss
Echium vulgare

A tall plant (up to 1 m) growing commonly on dunes. Its blue flowers are about 2 cm long and have protruding red stamens, making them resemble the tongues of vipers. The tall, stout stem has a spotted pattern and is bristly. The leaves grow at the base of the plant and wither as the plant flowers.

J	F	M	A	M	J	J	A	S	O	N	D

Eyebright

Euphrasia officinalis

A small plant growing in grassland, particularly dunes. The small stems are erect to a height of usually only a few centimetres. The white flowers, which are about 1 cm long, have a large lower lip with an orange spot in the centre as well as some purple lines. The leaves are hairy and jagged around the edge. Was once used as a treatment for eye conditions (and still is found in alternative therapies).

Yellow Rattle

Rhinanthus minor

An erect plant growing in grassland, particularly dunes. This is a semi-parasitic species taking some nutrients from grasses. The yellow flowers are about 1½ cm long, and each grow from within an inflated calyx. The leaves are pointed and toothed around the edge. The seeds inside the seedheads, when dry, rattle like a baby's toy.

J	F	M	A	M	J	J	A	S	O	N	D

J	F	M	A	M	J	J	A	S	O	N	D

Ragwort

Senecio jacobaea

A tall (up to about 1 m on dunes), erect plant growing commonly on all types of grassland. Has a distinctive head of yellow flowers, each one between 1 and 2½ cm across. Its leaves are hairy underneath, deeply lobed and irregularly toothed; they are often eaten by caterpillars, notably that of the cinnabar moth. Ragwort is poisonous and particularly dangerous to horses.

Pyramidal Orchid

Anacamptis pyrimidalis

A distinctive species of orchid because of the colour and shape of its flower spike. The flowers are reddish-purple and grow in a conical shape, particularly in the early stages of its growth. Its leaves are typically narrow and unspotted. The pyramidal orchid grows quite commonly on sand dunes.

| J | F | M | A | M | J | J | A | S | O | N | D |

| J | F | M | A | M | J | J | A | S | O | N | D |

Southern Marsh Orchid
Dactylorhiza praetermissa
The southern marsh orchid is a pinkish-purple orchid whose flowers grow in a dense, cylindrical shape. Can grow to as much as 80 cm tall. The leaves are usually unspotted. Grows on grassland and dunes, particularly where it is damp. (CH)

Autumn Lady's Tresses
Spiranthes spiralis
A wonderfully intricate little flower, but so very easy to pass by. It grows fairly widely on grassland, particularly the dunes of Upton Towans. It is very small, usually growing to about 10 cm tall. The tiny white flowers grow in a spiral fashion around the stem (which is downy and grey-green), bringing to mind a lady's hairstyle.

| J | F | M | A | M | J | J | A | S | O | N | D |

| J | F | M | A | M | J | J | A | S | O | N | D |

Marram Grass

Ammophila arenaria

There are not many species of grass that are found only on the coast, but the marram grass is found exclusively on sand dunes. Its root system helps to stabilize the dunes because it is so very extensive. Its leaves are very tough, and are rolled along their length to conserve water. Its colour is grey-green, and its flower spikes occur in the summer.

| J | F | M | A | M | J | J | A | S | O | N | D |

The Strandline

This section includes shells and the remains of other creatures that, in my experience, are more commonly seen washed up on beaches than in their natural state.

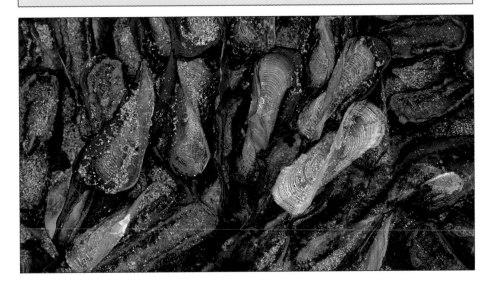

By-the-wind-sailor
Velella velella
When at sea this species has blue jelly tentacles hanging from a flat disc of cartilage. When washed up on the shore, the jelly soon decays, to leave a flat oval of cartilage with a semi-circular 'sail' of cartilage standing up on top. The 'sail' moves the animal around in the wind, but during autumnal storms hundreds of thousands can be washed up on the shore line. Size up to approximately 10 cm long.

Sea Potato Urchin
Echinocardium cordatum
This heart-shaped species of urchin lives buried in the sand, and is yellow when alive. Its brittle shell is sometimes washed ashore and deposited along strandlines. Size up to about 8 cm across.

Common Starfish
Asterias rubens
The common starfish can be found on any type of beach, but is most commonly found washed up on sandy beaches. Grows up to about 50 cm across.

Eggs of Common Whelk

Buccinum undatum

These spongy egg-case structures are the eggs of the common whelk. Each of the small cases may have contained a dozen or so eggs, only one of which is likely to have developed into a whelk. Total size about 10 cm across.

Goose Barnacle

Lepas anatifera

The goose barnacle lives its life far out at sea, but can get washed ashore during storms, particularly in autumn, because it attaches itself to floating debris. Usually found in large colonies, the creature has a retractable stalk and a blue-grey, yellow-edged shell. Shell up to 4 cm across.

Compass Jellyfish

Chrysaora hysoscella

Several species of jellyfish can be found in Cornish waters. All have a jelly-like body, and usually have tentacles with which they catch plankton. The compass jellyfish, illustrated here, grows up to 30 cm across. On the upper surface it has red-brown markings radiating from the centre.

Egg Case of Dogfish

Scyliorhinus caniculus

The egg case of a dogfish is commonly known as a mermaid's purse, due to its bulbous egg sack and long curling tendrils, which resemble purse strings.

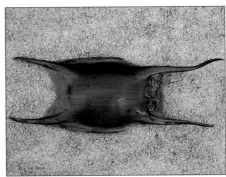

Egg Case of Spotted Ray
Raja montagui

The egg cases of rays do not have the tendrils of the dogfish's egg cases. They do, however, have 'horns'. In the spotted ray, the smaller horns often curl up, giving the impression of a sledge. The length, without horns, is up to 8 cm.

Egg Case of White Skate
Rostroraja alba

The egg cases of skates are generally more robust than those of the rays. That of the white skate can be as long as 18 cm without the horns. Its longer horns are flat and wide, while its shorter horns can be slightly hooked inwards at the end.

Cuttlefish Bone
Sepia officinalis
This is the internal float of the cuttlefish. During life it is filled with air to give the cuttlefish buoyancy, and it provides the creature with a skeleton.

Razorshell
Ensis ensis
A long, slim bivalve (two-shelled creature). The razorshell burrows quite deeply into sand, coming closer to the surface when covered in sea water to filter-feed. Can grow to about 15 cm long; other types of razorshell can grow a little longer. Commonly found washed up on sandy beaches.

Cockle

Cerastoderma edule

A bulbous-bodied bivalve (two-shelled creature). The common cockle has heavy ribbing from its hinge to the curved outer edge; across the ribbing are concentric growth rings. Cockles are burrowing creatures, living in sand, and are only commonly found washed ashore. This species can grow to about 5 cm long, though others can reach 10 cm.

Flat Periwinkle

Littorina fabalis (previously *Littorina mariae*)

Periwinkles are conspicuous because of their bright colours, but distinguishing between the many varieties is difficult. The flat periwinkle has a flattened spire, whereas most other types have a pointed apex. Typically about 1½ cm across. Can be found feeding on seaweeds, or washed up on sandy beaches.

Estuary and Creek (ES)

Cornwall doesn't have the vast estuaries and salt marshes associated with many other, flatter parts of Britain. One reason for this is the lack of a large landmass within the county and, therefore, its relatively short rivers. Another is the hard rock on which Cornwall is made: granite is not easily eroded by rivers, hence the rivers carry relatively little load to deposit at their mouths.

The longest river to which we have access is the Tamar, and though this is only half Cornish it does have fairly extensive mudflats and salt marshes on our side of the border, such as those owned by the Cornwall Wildlife Trust near Landulph. The longest river completely contained within the county is the Fowey, which lacks any significant areas of salt marsh, but at low tide offers good feeding to wading birds. The Camel Estuary offers excellent wildlife watching, and is very accessible along the Camel Trail between Padstow and Wadebridge, where there are extensive salt marshes and huge areas of mud exposed at low tide. We also have the Gannel Estuary – quite a sandy one this, but with a good range of salt marsh plants in accessible spots.

The largest areas of salt marsh on the Fal Estuary are near Ruan Lanihorne, and at the upper end of Restronguet Creek near Devoran. The Hayle Estuary is probably the most famous in the county for birdwatching, its geographical position making it a magnet for rare birds. Adjacent to this estuary at Ryan's Field there is a large area which is reverting to salt marsh under the ownership of the Royal Society for the Protection of Birds.

What Cornwall does have and which, to some extent, helps to define the county, is creeks with their characteristic overhanging oak trees. The mystical feel of a tidal creek at first light when mist clings to the trees helps us to imagine the secretive uses that our forebears may have had for these out-of-the-way places. The south coast of the county is dotted with such creeks; nowhere are there better examples than around the Fal, particularly around the Helford where there is a Voluntary Marine Conservation Area with a very active conservation group.

It is interesting to reflect on the formation of these creeks, since they are not the same

Right: The Gannel Estuary near Newquay

type of estuary that is found in the rest of the country. Their creation, in the form that we see today, is a story of climate change. Initially rivers created the valleys which were lined, quite naturally, with oak trees. In the period since the last Ice Age, about 10,000 years ago, the sea levels have risen so far that some of these valleys are flooded by salt water at high tides. The result is a unique environment where mature oak trees dip their branches into the sea and their roots penetrate earth which is smothered by seaweed. These flooded valleys have a name: they are called *rias*, and though they are not quite unique to Cornwall, they are very much a part of its history and natural history.

There are some special flowers which are associated with estuaries; many of these grow on salt marshes and flower during the summer, but the main interest in this habitat in Cornwall is during winter, when our creeks and estuaries come alive with waders fleeing the colder temperatures of more northerly and easterly climes. Actually that is only partly true, since we have a wider range of wading birds in autumn and spring than we do in winter, due to many species migrating through the county, only some of which stop for the winter. 'Autumn' for a wader is surprisingly early – the return from Arctic breed-

ing grounds starts in July for many birds. Migration continues through to October, with different species peaking at different times. A greater number of fewer species stay on for the winter, but this can be a very atmospheric time with large numbers of curlews, for example, gathering together for safety.

Watching waders requires some understanding of their behaviour and their environment. Given the choice, a wading bird would prefer to stay a long way from the shore where it can feed and stay safe from most predators. As the tide rises the waders are forced out of the low-lying creeks and closer to the shore. At high tide any suitable mud will be covered by seawater, and birds must retire to areas of land above the high-tide mark. For these reasons, the best time for watching such birds is on a rising tide; but before high tide, usually about two hours before, is a good time to start.

Some locations, such as the Hayle Estuary, can be good at high tide. Here during high spring tides birds are forced off the whole estuary and on to Ryan's Field, where there is a comfortable hide from which to watch them. At other states of the tide this field can be almost lifeless, partly due to the high levels of heavy metals in the substrate making this a fairly unproductive feeding area. It may seem surprising to us that any part of an estuary can be regarded as a productive feeding area, but it is a fact that a square metre of mud in an estuary contains a higher calorific value of food than any other environment on earth! The food isn't normally very appetizing to us, but there is a huge variety of crustacea as well as a good supply of worms. Take a close look at the wading birds feeding on the estuary and you will see that each is designed for feeding in a slightly different way, so that they don't all compete for the same food. The curlew has a long, down-curved bill; the godwit's is long and straight; the avocet's is up-curved; the dunlin's is shorter; the oystercatcher's is stout and straight. This is a great place to see the outcome of evolution!

Creek at Tresillian

Estuary and Creek Species

Otter
Lutra lutra

The otter is usually associated with fresh water, but can be found in estuaries. Best looked for at dusk on a calm evening when the ripples of a surfacing otter are more obvious. The otter is a big mammal, with a strong flexible body and long tail. Its fur is dark brown all over. The upper reaches of the Camel Estuary is probably the best place in Cornwall for otters.

Little Grebe
Tachybaptus ruficolis

The only common small grebe which, in winter, frequents estuaries; in summer it moves to fresh-water lakes to breed. In summer has chestnut neck, cream chin spot, dark back and head and pale, fluffy flanks and tail. In winter has dark brown wings and head, but buff otherwise. At all times of year the shape of this bird is distinctive: short neck; small head; rounded body and fluffed out pale rump. Very active, continually diving, and always dives to avoid danger. Photo: summer plumage.

| J | F | M | A | M | J | J | A | S | O | N | D |

| J | F | M | A | M | J | J | A | S | O | N | D |

Cormorant
Phalocrocorax carbo

The cormorant is much more inclined to inhabit estuaries and inland waterways than the similar shag. It is larger than the shag, with a white throat patch in all stages of plumage except juvenile. Adults in spring have a white thigh patch. Bill and head shape are bigger than in shag. When diving, the cormorant slips under water without a pronounced jump. Shares the shag's habit of holding its wings out to dry. (CH)

Grey Heron
Ardea cinerea

A very large wading bird. Grey wings and white neck; head decorated with a black crown stripe and yellow bill. Usually nests in trees, though at Marazion nests in reed bed. Stalks slowly and patiently for fish and a multitude of other prey. Can be found at freshwater locations as well as on estuaries.

| J | F | M | A | M | J | J | A | S | O | N | D |

| J | F | M | A | M | J | J | A | S | O | N | D |

Little Egret
Egretta garzetta
Smaller than a grey heron, with all white plumage. Has white nape plumes and other ornate plumes on back during breeding season. Legs are black, but feet are yellow. Has a more active feeding behaviour than the grey heron, usually takes small fish. Nests in trees and generally feeds in estuaries, though will sometimes take to rock pools and other beaches. (RP)

Mute Swan
Cygnus olor
An easily identified bird, the only possible confusion species are two other species of swan (Bewick's and whooper), which occur only very rarely during the winter. The mute swan has an orange-red bill; the male has a black knob above it. Juveniles, or cygnets, are brown, gradually moulting into adult plumage after a year. Commonly found at estuaries, otherwise inland on fresh-water ways.

J	F	M	A	M	J	J	A	S	O	N	D

J	F	M	A	M	J	J	A	S	O	N	D

Shelduck

Tadorna tadorna

This is our largest duck. Basically white body with a brown breast band and dark green head. The black wing feathers give it a pied appearance from a distance. Has a red bill (on which the male has a knob) and pink legs. Breeds mostly in woodlands adjacent to muddy creeks. Can be found throughout the year, but is uncommon in late summer when shelducks migrate to moulting areas out of county (probably Bridgwater Bay).

Mallard

Anas platyrhynchos

This is the archetypal duck, commonly seen on duck ponds. Can frequently be seen in estuaries. Male has green head, grey body and brown breast; female is brown. In summer they moult, when they become flightless and drab brown.

| J | F | M | A | M | J | J | A | S | O | N | D |

| J | F | M | A | M | J | J | A | S | O | N | D |

Wigeon
Anas penelope

Wigeon visit Cornwall in winter, when they are extremely numerous on estuaries. The male, or drake, is quite colourful, with a brick-red head, yellow forehead, grey body and black tail. Females are brown, but can be distinguished from other species by their petite head shape, and by the fact that they mix with male wigeon! Frequently call and make a distinctive whistling 'wee-oooo' sound. A little smaller than a mallard. Photo: male.

Teal
Anas crecca

A very small duck. Males are colourful with an intricate pattern of red, green and cream face markings, grey body and cream rump. Females are brown, but with a green wing patch. Frequent on estuaries in winter along with wigeon. Photo: male.

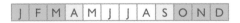

| J | F | M | A | M | J | J | A | S | O | N | D |

| J | F | M | A | M | J | J | A | S | O | N | D |

Oystercatcher

Haematopus ostralegus

The oystercatcher is one of the most obvious of all waders, being large and black and white with an obvious red bill and pinkish legs. Plumage changes slightly in winter, when adult birds develop a white chin stripe. Breeds in small numbers around the rocky coasts of Cornwall, when it can be very vociferous in defence of its territory. Its voice consists of shrill peeps and excited 'klip-klip-klip' notes. In winter is more numerous and is found mostly on estuaries. (CH, SD, RP)

J F M A M J J A S O N D

Avocet
Recurvirostra avosetta

The avocet is an elegant wading bird. Mostly white in plumage, but with black markings on its wings and head. It has a black, up-turned bill with which it sifts through the water's surface with a sweeping motion. Only occurs in winter when it is almost always found in flocks. Is only regular on the Tamar estuary around Cargreen.

Golden Plover
Pluvialis apricaria

A medium-sized wader, gold-spangled brown on its back and buff below. In summer plumage it has a black belly and face; we may see some individuals with remnants of this plumage in spring and autumn. Always occurs in flocks, and often associates with lapwings. Feeds on estuaries at low tide, and often moves to farmland at high tide. Has a plaintive 'peeyou' call. Photo: winter plumage.

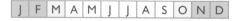

| J | F | M | A | M | J | J | A | S | O | N | D |

| J | F | M | A | M | J | J | A | S | O | N | D |

Grey Plover

Pluvialis squatarola

The grey plover is similar in size to the golden plover, but is more often seen in small groups or singly. Plumage is a much colder grey-brown than in the golden plover, and in flight its black axillaries, or armpits, are obvious. Photo: winter plumage. (RP, CH)

Lapwing

Vanellus vanellus

The lapwing is a medium-sized wader with a wonderfully buoyant flight. From a distance appears to be black and white, but close up it has a green back, russet rump, black and white face markings and a black crest. Sometimes associates with golden plovers; can be found on estuaries, marsh and arable land. Has a distinctive 'peewit' call.

| J | F | M | A | M | J | J | A | S | O | N | D |

| J | F | M | A | M | J | J | A | S | O | N | D |

Dunlin

Calidris alpina

The dunlin is a small wader. In winter it has a grey back and white belly with some streaking on the upper breast. In summer is brown on the back with a black belly. Can show variable streaking on its flanks. Its bill is of medium length and is down-curved. Common on estuaries. Usually occurs in flocks. Photo: summer plumage. (CH, RP, SD)

Black-tailed Godwit

Limosa limosa

The black-tailed godwit is a large wading bird with long legs and a long straight (if anything slightly up-turned) bill. Only common in winter when it is brown with a paler belly, white rump, black tail and a black and white wing pattern when seen in flight. Frequently seen on muddy creeks. Only confusable with the bar-tailed godwit, which lacks the distinctive tail and wing pattern of the black-tailed godwit. Photo: winter plumage.

| J | F | M | A | M | J | J | A | S | O | N | D |

| J | F | M | A | M | J | J | A | S | O | N | D |

Whimbrel

Numenius phaeopus

The whimbrel resembles a small curlew, but has a much shorter, more steeply down-curved bill. Only occurs in any numbers on migration, when it can be seen anywhere around the coast from fields to estuaries to beaches. Has a very distinctive call consisting of a high pitched 'kee-hee-hee'. At close quarters look for the white crown and eye stripes. (CH, RP, SD)

Curlew

Numenius arquata

A large wading bird, the curlew is brown all over except for a white rump, only visible in flight. It is the long, down-curved bill which makes this bird exceptional. Has a wonderfully evocative call consisting of bubbling 'cur-lee' notes. Found on estuaries in winter, and breeds in very small numbers on moorland.

| J | F | M | A | M | J | J | A | S | O | N | D |

| J | F | M | A | M | J | J | A | S | O | N | D |

Redshank

Tringa totanus

Red legs and a straight red bill make this medium-sized wader stand out. Otherwise its plumage is a fairly plain, streaky brown. In flight white markings on the rump and wings become apparent. Found in small flocks on estuaries and creeks. Quite a noisy bird, frequently the first wader to warn of danger with a 'tyou-you' call.

Greenshank

Tringa nebularia

Slightly larger than the redshank, and with long, grey-green legs and slightly up-turned bill. In winter the greenshank has white belly and dark wings, making it look definitely two-tone, unlike the much browner redshank. In flight it reveals its white rump but plain dark wings. Most common on muddy creeks.

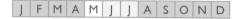

Common Sandpiper

Actitis hypoleucos

A small wader with brown back and white belly, the common sandpiper has a clearly defined brown bib. The most obvious feature is the constant bobbing action. In flight it has an unusual flicking wing beat, and flies low over the surface of the water. Found mostly on migration around estuaries and lakes.

Black-headed Gull

Larus ridibundus

The black-headed gull is a small gull with grey back and white belly and neck. In summer it has a chocolate-brown face, whereas in winter it has a dark smudge behind the eye. In flight its wings have a white leading edge. Legs and bill are deep red. Photo: summer plumage.

| J | F | M | A | M | J | J | A | S | O | N | D |

Lesser Black-backed Gull
Larus fuscus

A large gull with dark grey wings and white belly and head. Similar to the great black-backed gull from which it differs in being slightly smaller, slightly less dark, and with yellow legs. Bill is yellow with red tip. Adults develop some streaking on the head in winter. Juveniles are brown and take three years to develop adult plumage. Can be seen most commonly on estuaries in winter. (CH)

Herring Gull
Larus argentatus

The archetypal seaside gull. Grey back and white belly and head. Bill is yellow with a red tip, legs are pink. In winter adults develop a well-streaked head. Juveniles are brown and take three years to develop adult plumage. Nests commonly in seaside towns, and can be seen on estuaries in winter. (CH, RP)

| J | F | M | A | M | J | J | A | S | O | N | D |

| J | F | M | A | M | J | J | A | S | O | N | D |

Great Black-backed Gull
Larus marinus

This is the largest of our gulls. Very dark wings and pink legs. Found around harbour towns throughout the year, and on estuaries in the winter. In winter adults may develop slight streaking on the head. Juveniles are brown and take three years to develop adult plumage. (CH)

Kingfisher
Alcedo atthis

Although associated with fresh water, the kingfisher can often be seen around estuaries in winter. A fairly obvious bird with orange belly and blue wings and head. Much smaller than many people expect, not much bigger than a chaffinch. Flies low over water making a thin whistling 'seee' call.

| J | F | M | A | M | J | J | A | S | O | N | D |

| J | F | M | A | M | J | J | A | S | O | N | D |

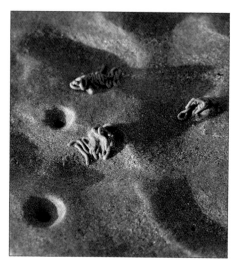

Lugworm
Arenicola marina

The lugworm lives on muddy estuaries and some sandy beaches. Its presence can be determined by the holes and worm casts which are adjacent to each other on the surface of the beach, and which mark the entrances to its U-shaped burrow. (SD)

Sea Purslane
Halimione portulacoides

A sprawling, grey-green plant of salt marshes and tidal creeks. The tiny flowers are yellow but insignificant. Leaves are elliptical and fleshy. Usually about 40 cm tall, though can reach up to 80 cm. Not particularly attractive, but distinctive because of its grey-green leaves.

| J | F | M | A | M | J | J | A | S | O | N | D |

Glasswort or Marsh Samphire

Salicornia europaea

A small, erect and succulent plant of salt marshes. The flowers are tiny, almost microscopic. The leaves are simply a continuation of the stem, in shape and structure. Can be eaten if picked in the spring.

Golden Samphire

Inula crithmoides

A fairly tall (up to 1 m), fleshy-leaved plant of salt marshes and other coastal areas. Leaves, as well as being succulent, are narrow and linear. The yellow flowers are about 2 ½ cm across. (CH)

J	F	M	A	M	J	J	A	S	O	N	D

J	F	M	A	M	J	J	A	S	O	N	D

Common Scurvygrass

Cochleria officinalis

A sprawling plant often covering large areas on saltmarshes, coastal fields and hedgebanks. The small white flowers (up to 1 cm across) are sometimes washed with pink, and have four petals. The dark green leaves are fleshy and heart-shaped. (CH)

| J | F | M | A | M | J | J | A | S | O | N | D |

Cliff and Heath (CH)

The majority of the coastline of Cornwall is made up of rocky cliffs, with a coast path that winds its way up and down, back and forth, with every twist and turn in the shape of the coast. This coastline has been created by a battle between the rock which forms the land, and the sea, which does its best to erode every weakness it can find. Over time, the shape of the coastline changes, creating in Cornwall some of the most wondrous and breathtaking seascapes in the whole of the UK.

Cornwall has a more dramatic coastline than any other English county because of the incredibly erosive effect of the ocean. The county is affected by huge waves, created in the Atlantic and whipped up by strong winds that blow from the same direction as the dominant ocean current. The waves are uninterrupted by land in a way in which the rest of England does not experience. This long 'fetch', as it is known by geographers, is not only responsible for the dramatic creation of our coastline, but also the waves which attract so many surfers here throughout the year.

The elements that contribute to the appeal of our coastline include cliffs, headlands, sea stacks, arches, caves, blowholes, coves and islands, all of which are formed by the forces of the ocean. Cliffs are simply carved out of the rock by a straightforward competition between ocean and land. Headlands are formed where more solid sections of rock withstand the beating for longer than the surrounding rocks. Sea stacks, such as those very famous ones at Bedruthan, are formed when the sea exploits cracks and weaknesses around a pinnacle of rock, leaving it standing proud of the cliffs. Often an arch will form before the roof collapses to leave a freestanding stack. Caves are created where joints between rock types, or weaknesses at the foot of a cliff, allow the waves to cut into the rock face, undermining the cliff. Waves breaking into a cave have to find a way out, and sometimes the only way is up. Such circumstances can lead to holes appearing up to a few hundred metres inland of the cliff edge. Gradually the roof of the cave collapses, leaving a bridge on the cliff top, and so a 'blowhole' is formed. After time the bridge may collapse, leaving a large inlet or cove behind.

Arches, caves and stacks have been created by the forces of the ocean: a view near Basset's Cove (near Portreath)

The cliffs and rocks which resist the effects of the sea are inhabited by a special mix of wildlife. Here we find nesting seabirds such as kittiwakes, guillemots, razorbills and fulmars; even a few puffins are left on isolated islands. It is unlikely that the pigeons we see nesting here are genuinely of a wild stock, but the peregrines, which also live on the cliffs and hunt them, don't mind that! Other birds which nest on the cliffs include ravens and, of course, the famous choughs. The colour of the rocks is often altered completely by a covering of lichens. Look carefully and you will notice that close to the sea's edge the lichens are black and thinly encrusting the rock's surface; further away from the effect of the sea, the lichen is slightly more leafy and very yellow; higher still and there are more luxuriant forms which come in a grey-green colour.

On top of the cliffs, behind the beaches, around the coast path we have a wide range of vegetation between the cliff edge and the land which is cultivated. Though the habitats along this strip of land are diverse, I refer to it all as 'coastal heath'.

Some of this coastal heath is dominated by traditional dry heathland species, including heather and gorse. Many of the finest examples, such as those around St Agnes Head, grow in association with old mining sites. Very few plants can cope with the highly acidic nature of the thin, gravely soils left behind when mining ceased. Heather, bell heather and western gorse certainly can, but even they are kept in check by the elements.

In other parts of the coast we have wonderful areas of wildflowers. The grasses here are kept at bay by wind and sea spray, to allow an annual bounty of wildflowers which create a wonderful display every spring and summer. Flowers which typify this environment include thrift, sea campion, kidney vetch and bird's-foot trefoil.

For most of the last 2,000 years or so our coastline was grazed by domesticated animals. This practice ceased at around the time of the Second World War, because people working the land had to concentrate on increasing productivity and the coastline was never very productive. In the second half of the twentieth century the balance of flowers and scrub on the coast changed slightly. Despite the effects of the wind and salt spray, some species of scrub have been gradually encroaching into areas previously dominated by flowers. To address this balance, organizations with a keen interest in the protection of our coastline, such as the National Trust, have begun to reintroduce coastal grazing.

The breeds which are being used are necessarily old breeds of cattle, pony and sheep. More modern breeds cannot cope with the coarse grazing and dangerous conditions. We can now see Dartmoor ponies at Rame Head; Highland cattle above Kynance Cove; Longhorn cattle at Nanjulian; Red Devon cattle at Boscastle, and Shetland ponies at Predannack Cliffs, to name but a few. After just a few years of grazing, the difference in the growth of flowers can be astonishing. In most cases the coastal heath is grazed during autumn and winter, allowing the spring and summer flowers to grow and set seed undisturbed. So some of the main beneficiaries of such grazing are flowers such as spring squill, heath spotted orchid, wild thyme and sheep's bit scabious, to name but a few.

If it were not for the reintroduction of grazing animals, the small population of choughs which re-established themselves around the Lizard might not have been successful. The chough likes to feed on short turf, and often associates with cattle, feeding on larvae around their dung. Other creatures, such as the insects that feed and lay their eggs on the wildflowers of the coast are also beneficiaries of this renewed activity.

Cliff and Heath Species

Fox

Vulpes vulpes

The fox is a frequent hunter on the coast of Cornwall, where the vegetation is often long enough to host its prey. Dawn and dusk are the best times to see this predator, and summer is the best time of year since they will have cubs to feed. Look for them basking in the early morning sun. (ES, SD)

Badger

Meles meles

Badgers are often associated with woodland, but the large entrance holes to their setts can be found around the coast too. Distinguish a badger hole from a large rabbit hole by a mound of earth at the entrance. There may also be badger latrines, which are often small holes filled with dark faeces.

J	F	M	A	M	J	J	A	S	O	N	D

J	F	M	A	M	J	J	A	S	O	N	D

Bottlenose Dolphin
Tursiops truncatus

Bottlenose dolphins are regularly seen around the coast of Cornwall, but are difficult to predict. These dolphins live close to shore and often leap out of the water either in play or as a hunting strategy. They can be seen at any time of year, and St Ives Bay is as good a place as any to look.

Grey Seal
Halichoerus grypus

Grey seals are the only species of seal that occurs regularly in Cornwall, and they are widespread around the county. They can be seen at any time of year almost exclusively around rocky shorelines. The most frequent sighting is of a head bobbing above the water, but they do come ashore to haul out on rocks and beaches to bask and give birth.

| J | F | M | A | M | J | J | A | S | O | N | D |

| J | F | M | A | M | J | J | A | S | O | N | D |

Basking Shark
Cetorhinus maximus

Basking sharks can be seen around Cornwall typically in the early summer. The best locations seem to be along the south coast, between Porthcurno and the Lizard. They eat plankton by swimming through the water with their huge mouths open. From above the water's surface we see a tail and dorsal fin.

Shag
Phalocrocorax aristotelis

The shag is closely related to the cormorant, but is more frequently seen around rocky coasts. The shag is smaller and daintier in proportion. In breeding plumage the shag has a crest. Adult plumage appears to be black but actually has a green gloss. Juveniles are brown and have a paler belly. Can be distinguished from a cormorant by the way it dives for fish: the shag always jumps as it dives.

| J | F | M | A | M | J | J | A | S | O | N | D |

| J | F | M | A | M | J | J | A | S | O | N | D |

Fulmar

Fulmarus glacialis

The fulmar resembles a gull but is actually more closely related to the shearwaters and petrels. It has a very characteristic flight on straight, stiff wings, often gliding for great distances without flapping. It nests on cliff ledges and can be found around the entire coast of Cornwall.

Gannet

Morus bassanus

The gannet is a huge seabird with a wing span of up to 2 m. Adults are white with a yellow head and black wing tips; young birds are brown at first, gradually changing to adult plumage over four years. Their technique of plunge-diving makes them an impressive bird to watch. The nearest breeding colony is in Wales; they are most frequently seen during stormy weather. Photo: adult.

| J | F | M | A | M | J | J | A | S | O | N | D |

| J | F | M | A | M | J | J | A | S | O | N | D |

Buzzard
Buteo buteo

The buzzard is Cornwall's largest resident bird of prey. Not just a bird of the coast, but it is often found there. The buzzard is usually dark brown with a paler breast band. Some individuals, often juveniles, are much paler, showing varying amounts of white or cream in their plumage. Its call is a loud mewing. Usually sits on telegraph poles looking for prey, but around the coast will try to hover into a stiff wind. (ES, SD)

Peregrine Falcon
Falco peregrinus

The peregrine is slate grey above and streaked below, with an obvious black mask and moustache. It is slightly bigger than the kestrel, but is much bulkier with a barrel-breast. Its tail and wings are shorter in proportion to its body size than those of the kestrel. It preys on birds by flying high and swooping on them from above; the most frequent prey is probably the pigeon. (ES, SD)

Kestrel
Falco tinnunculus
The kestrel is the only bird of prey that can truly hover, and this is what the kestrel does, habitually. It has long wings and tail, a ginger-brown back, and spotted chest. Males are a little more colourful than females, having a grey head and tail. Its wing shape can vary from pointed to very rounded, depending upon its flight. (ES, SD)

Kittiwake
Rissa tridactyla
The kittiwake is a small, dainty gull which shuns human attention. Nests in colonies on cliffs around the county, where it can be heard calling its name 'kitti-waaaake'. In flight it has black wing tips and two-tone grey wings. Juveniles have a black 'W' across their wings.

J F M A M J J A S O N D

J F M A M J J A S O N D

Guillemot

Uria aalge

Guillemots nest in colonies on precipitous cliff ledges. They are most numerous on the north coast, and can be seen well on the islands between Boscastle and Tintagel. Has dark brown back and head and a white belly. Stance is often upright when on land. Swims on the surface of the sea in groups, and dives by swimming into the water. Has small wings that whirr in flight. In winter its cheeks become white and it spends time further out to sea, except in storms when it can be forced close to land. Photo: summer plumage.

Razorbill

Alca torda

Distribution and behaviour very similar to guillemot. Differences include: razor-shaped bill with white lines along and across it; darker plumage on back, and nests in holes among rocks as well as on ledges. Photo: summer plumage.

Puffin

Fratercula arctica

Now very uncommon around the Cornish coast, puffins can still be found on Scilly and one or two remote islands. Seeing them from the Cornish coast path is a challenge. The best place is probably 'The Mouls', an island visible from Pentire Head; good binoculars will be needed. Only occasionally seen around the coast in winter, never as common as guillemot and razorbill. Photo: summer plumage.

Feral Pigeon/Rock Dove

Columba livia

The rock dove was once a pure species found around the coast of Cornwall, but it has interbred with feral pigeons to the extent that it no longer exists in its own right. The purest forms have a white rump, visible in flight, otherwise pale grey with darker head and a pink and green suffusion around the neck.

J	F	M	A	M	J	J	A	S	O	N	D

J	F	M	A	M	J	J	A	S	O	N	D

Rock Pipit

Anthus petrosus

A small, sooty-brown bird with a smudgy, streaked breast and flanks. On closer inspection has a creamy white supercilium (stripe over eye). Similar to meadow pipit, which is found on grassland, but darker, smudgier plumage and dark legs help to identify this species. Usually found on rocky coasts; has an attractive song flight which involves parachuting from the sky while singing. (RP)

Meadow Pipit

Anthus pratensis

A common bird of grassland around the coast as well as inland. Buff-coloured underneath with dark spots which often amalgamate into a cluster in the centre of the breast. Its back is brown with streaking. Has a thin, weak 'tsip-tsip' call in flight. Much warmer toned than the rock pipit, as well as being slightly smaller and slimmer. (SD)

J	F	M	A	M	J	J	A	S	O	N	D

J	F	M	A	M	J	J	A	S	O	N	D

Wheatear

Oenanthe oenanthe

Most commonly seen as a migratory bird in spring and autumn on rocky coastlines. Habitually perches briefly on rocks and fence posts where it often flicks its tail. Males have grey back, pale belly, black mask and dark wings; females are a warm brown with slightly greyer back and darker wings. Male and female have a white rump and tail with a terminal dark band; the flash of white created by the tail in flight is quite distinctive. Photo: female. (SD)

Stonechat

Saxicola torquata

Probably our most obvious small bird of the coast, due to its habit of sitting on the tops of bushes and fence posts all the time. Males are very striking with dark brown back, rosy red breast, black head and white collar; females have a hint of red in their breast but are otherwise mostly brown. Has a distinctive call which sounds like two pebbles being tapped together. Photo: male. (SD)

| J | F | M | A | M | J | J | A | S | O | N | D |

| J | F | M | A | M | J | J | A | S | O | N | D |

Whitethroat

Sylvia communis

A very numerous warbler found in scrubby vegetation around the coast. Males and females are brown with a white throat patch; males also have a grey head. Most obvious in May and June, when males sit on top of bushes to sing, otherwise extremely secretive. The song is quite scratchy, and is interspersed with various 'churrs and gurrrs'. Has an attractive song flight in which males flutter down to a perch while singing. Photo: male.

Chough

Pyrrhocorax pyrrhocorax

The chough was extinct throughout the second half of the twentieth century, but now has established an increasing breeding population based initially on a single pair near Lizard Point. Can now be found along the coast between the Lizard and West Penwith. Has a glossy black plumage with red legs and bill. In flight it has splayed wing tips, and frequently calls 'chiow'. Similar size to jackdaw.

J	F	M	A	M	J	J	A	S	O	N	D

J	F	M	A	M	J	J	A	S	O	N	D

Raven
Corvus corax
A very large member of the crow family, the raven is even bigger than a buzzard. Best identified by listening to its calls, which consist of a variety of honks and 'kraaaks'. Has a big shaggy neck with heavy bill. In flight its tail is long and wedge-shaped at the tip. Its wings often look a little swept back. Nests on cliffs making a huge, messy nest.

Jackdaw
Corvus monedula
The jackdaw is a common bird of the coast, often occurring in large flocks. Nests in holes in the cliffs as well as in the chimneys of nearby houses. Basically a black bird, but with a grey neck and dark forehead. Has a variety of calls, but most frequent are a drawn out 'kyaaa' and harsh 'kyack'.

| J | F | M | A | M | J | J | A | S | O | N | D |

| J | F | M | A | M | J | J | A | S | O | N | D |

Common Lizard
Lacerta vivipara
The common lizard is widespread across the county, and is quite numerous around the coast, because of the suitable habitat; but even here it is very difficult to see. A scuttling sound in the vegetation as we pass by is the only evidence most of us will have of a common lizard, but they are creatures of habit so try waiting and it might re-emerge to bask again. (SD)

Linnet
Carduelis cannabina
A common finch found particularly in association with gorse, where it nests. Males have a rosy breast and forehead contrasting with a grey head and ginger back; females are brown with a streaked breast. Has a very attractive metallic twittering song. Almost always seen in small flocks, and usually calls in flight. Photo: male. (ES, SD)

| J | F | M | A | M | J | J | A | S | O | N | D |

| J | F | M | A | M | J | J | A | S | O | N | D |

Slow Worm
Anguis fragilis

Slow worms are a type of reptile closely related to the common lizard. They have evolved without legs but otherwise are similar to lizards. Males are grey, females are bronze with darker brown flanks. They tend to hide underneath logs and stones, but sometimes come out to bask. Photo: male. (SD)

Adder
Vipera berus

The adder is our only poisonous snake, and is the only snake which is common around the coast of Cornwall. It is most often found among the heather of coastal heath and in the long grass of sand dunes. It has a distinctive zig-zag pattern along its back, which tends to be more of a black and white combination in males and two-tone brown in females. Photo: male. (SD)

| J | F | M | A | M | J | J | A | S | O | N | D |

| J | F | M | A | M | J | J | A | S | O | N | D |

Wall Brown

Lasiommata megera

The wall brown is a medium-sized butterfly. On upperwing is brown with a ginger pattern dotted with dark eye spots (one on forewing, three on hindwing), each of which has a small central white dot. The hind underwing is grey and brown and well camouflaged. Very common around the coast where rough grassland provides foodplants for its caterpillars and stone walls provide basking sites for the adults. Basks with wings half open.

Clouded Yellow

Colias croceus

The clouded yellow is a migrant butterfly which occasionally occurs in huge numbers around the coast. Classically seen in largest numbers during June and July and again in September, but in good years can be seen throughout the summer. Almost always rests and basks with its wings closed, revealing yellow with a light spot on the hindwing and dark spots on the forewing. The upperwings are more orangey in colour, with a dark smudgy margin. (SD)

J	F	M	A	M	J	J	A	S	O	N	D

J	F	M	A	M	J	J	A	S	O	N	D

Green Hairstreak

Callophrys rubi

The green hairstreak is a tiny butterfly. It is almost entirely iridescent green underneath. When at rest it keeps its wings closed, and looks very much like a leaf. Often associates with gorse and is quite territorial.

Six-spot Burnet Moth

Zygaena filipendulae

The six-spot burnet is a strikingly colourful day-flying moth found around the coast in association with bird's-foot trefoil on which it lays its eggs. Has a dark forewing (with a green sheen) with six red spots (two of which often seem to merge together); its hindwing is red. Often feeds on knapweed. (SD)

| J | F | M | A | M | J | J | A | S | O | N | D |

| J | F | M | A | M | J | J | A | S | O | N | D |

Emperor Moth

Saturnia pavonia

The emperor is a huge moth which lives on heathland. The female flies by night, while the male flies by day. Both are grey-brown with a huge eye-spot on each wing. The male's hindwing is orange-brown. It is more common to see the larva of this species as it crosses pathways. The young larva is black and hairy with orange spots; older larvae are green with yellow, black and orange spots. Photo: female.

Silver-Y Moth

Autographa gamma

The silver-Y moth is a migrant species, arriving on the coast in large numbers in suitable conditions. It flies by day and night, drinking from the flowers of any plants. Easily distinguished by the silvery-coloured Y-shape on each forewing. (SD)

| J | F | M | A | M | J | J | A | S | O | N | D |

| J | F | M | A | M | J | J | A | S | O | N | D |

Oak Eggar Moth

Lasiocampa quercus

The oak eggar is a large moth which flies by night and lives around heathland, often on the coast. The larvae are brown and furry with white spots on the flanks. Look out for the acorn-shaped, papery brown cocoons which are often scattered around on suitable habitat in summer (it is the acorn-shaped cocoons which are responsible for this species' name). Photos: adult and opened cocoons.

Oil Beetle

Meloe proscarabaeus

An oily black beetle with a huge, bulbous body. Found on grassland often near the coast. The oil beetle has a complex life cycle in which its larvae attach themselves to bees and are carried back to their nest where they are fed by the bee and eat the bee's larvae. (CH)

J	F	M	A	M	J	J	A	S	O	N	D

J	F	M	A	M	J	J	A	S	O	N	D

Hottentot Fig
Carprobrotus edulis
A creeping perennial of the coastline, the Hottentot fig has fleshy, succulent leaves with triangular cross-section. Flowers are large, up to 10 cm across, and can be yellow or pink/purple. It is a garden escape introduced from South Africa, and is now regarded as an invasive pest which smothers natural vegetation.

Sea Beet
Beta vulgaris
A fairly unattractive plant, vaguely reminiscent of dock. It grows up to about 80 cm tall, but often collapses in a sprawling mass. The leaves are shiny and slightly fleshy, usually elongated, wedge-shaped. Flowers are green and occur in spikes. Very common. (ES, SD)

| J | F | M | A | M | J | J | A | S | O | N | D |

| J | F | M | A | M | J | J | A | S | O | N | D |

Greater Sea Spurrey
Spergularia media

The greater sea spurrey is a small plant of rocky coasts and estuaries. It has a very small flower, about 1 cm across, with pale pink flowers. The petals are longer than the sepals, which helps to distinguish this from other sea spurreys. The leaves are narrow but fleshy. (ES)

Sea Campion
Silene maritima

The sea campion is a clump-forming plant, which grows in all coastal areas. Its white flowers, which are up to 2½ cm across, have a bladder-like calyx behind their petals, and its leaves are grey-green in colour. This plant is tolerant of some heavy metals, and can therefore be found growing on old mining sites. (ES, SD)

| J | F | M | A | M | J | J | A | S | O | N | D |

| J | F | M | A | M | J | J | A | S | O | N | D |

Black Mustard
Brassica nigra
A huge, bushy plant of hedgerows, black mustard is covered in flowers during the early summer. The flowers are yellow, and though they are individually small (up to 1 cm) they are borne in conspicuous clusters which create a mass of colour. Its lower leaves are large, bristly and lobed, with the end lobe being larger than the others. (SD)

Navelwort
Umbilicus rupestris
Most of the year navelwort is obvious only for its fleshy leaves, which have a dimple in the middle said to resemble a navel. In early summer a tall (10–80 cm) flower spike of small, greenish/yellow flowers emerges; this changes colour with age, and may redden before becoming dry and brown. Conspicuous because it often grows from walls and rock crevices where little else can grow.

J	F	M	A	M	J	J	A	S	O	N	D

J	F	M	A	M	J	J	A	S	O	N	D

English Stonecrop

Sedum anglicum

English stonecrop is a low, mat-forming plant. It has small flowers (approximately 1 cm across) which vary from white to pink. Its leaves are small and succulent. It grows on rocks and beside paths where other vegetation does not compete, and can cope with acidic conditions and ex-mining sites. (SD)

Burnet Rose

Rosa pimpinellifolia

The burnet rose tends to grow in small bushes, though it does climb. It has cream-coloured flowers which grow up to 4 cm across. Its leaves are comprised of from 6 to 11 leaflets, and its thorns are straight. Its hips are dark purple. It grows on rocky ground, and often on dunes. (SD)

| J | F | M | A | M | J | J | A | S | O | N | D |

| J | F | M | A | M | J | J | A | S | O | N | D |

Western Gorse
Ulex gallii

Western gorse is similar to European gorse, but does not grow to the same height, and is usually restricted to 1 m tall at most. It is best distinguished by the season in which it flowers, but its branches are never as long and leggy. Almost always grows among heather, where it is usually no taller than the surrounding vegetation. Photo: western gorse among heather.

Common Gorse
Ulex europaeus

A dense, spiny shrub growing up to 3 m tall, though rarely quite so high around the coast. Its yellow flowers are up to 2 cm long, and are strongly scented of coconut. The leaves are adapted as rigid spines. Its flattened black pods burst open with a cracking sound on hot summer days. Also known as furze. (ES, SD)

| J | F | M | A | M | J | J | A | S | O | N | D |

| J | F | M | A | M | J | J | A | S | O | N | D |

Dyer's Greenweed
Genista tinctoria

Dyer's greenweed grows on coastal heath, and is only obvious when its yellow flowers form. The small yellow flowers (which are about 1 ½ cm long) are borne in spikes. The leaves are lanceolate (shaped like a spearhead), and are often hairy.

Kidney Vetch
Anthyllis vulneraria

A short, sprawling plant of the coast, its flowers are individually small (about 1 ½ cm across), but are borne in paired heads. Each of the pair of flowers is kidney shaped, and it is rare for both to bloom at the same time. The flowers are yellow, but can be quite orange. There are 3–9 oval leaflets with each compound leaf, and these are silky and hairy. (SD)

J	F	M	A	M	J	J	A	S	O	N	D

J	F	M	A	M	J	J	A	S	O	N	D

Bloody Cranesbill

Geranium sanguineum

A hairy perennial often with stout woody stems growing to a height of about 50 cm. Flowers have five notched petals, and are a deep purple colour. The leaves are deeply divided into pointed lobes. Normally a lime-loving plant, the best location for this species in Cornwall is at Kynance Cove on the Lizard.

Common Mallow

Malva sylvestris

Usually a fairly bushy plant growing up to 1 m tall. Its large pinkish-purple flowers are about 3 or 4 cm across, and have five notched petals. Its leaves are rounded and are softly hairy. Found around the coast, often on sandy soil. (SD)

J	F	M	A	M	J	J	A	S	O	N	D

J	F	M	A	M	J	J	A	S	O	N	D

Milkwort

Polygala vulgaris

A very small insignificant plant of coastal heath, often in similar locations to lousewort. Its small flowers (abour ½ cm across) are blue or sometimes mauve and are borne in small, weak spikes. Its leaves are spear-head in shape.

J	F	M	A	M	J	J	A	S	O	N	D

Tamarisk

Tamarix gallica

An evergreen shrub growing to about 3 m tall, and quite bushy in structure with weeping branches. Its leaves are very small and scale-like. Flowers are pink occurring in spikes. Often occurs in hedgerows by the sea, particularly on sandy soils.

J	F	M	A	M	J	J	A	S	O	N	D

Rock Samphire
Crithmum maritimum
Fleshy and hairless, rock samphire can be seen commonly growing on rocks around the coast. Its flowers are greenish-yellow and grow in umbels (saucer-shaped heads) which have short, stout stems. The leaves are succulent, but long and pointed. (SD)

Wild Carrot
Daucus carota
Wild carrot is a common plant of grassland around the coast. Its white flowers grow in large heads which vary from saucer-shaped to almost spherical. Often the central flower in the head is sterile and of a different colour. Its leaves and stems are coarsely hairy, and smell of carrot when pressed. This is a sub-species of the garden carrot. (SD)

Heather

Calluna vulgaris

Sometimes known as 'ling', this is the commonest species of heather around the coast. It has very small, light pink flowers which grow in spikes, and tiny, thin leaves. The wonderful effect of heather is created by the mass of flowers which often occur together.

Bell Heather

Erica cinerea

Bell heather is often found in association with heather. Its flowers are slightly larger, and are a much deeper purple in colour. The individual flowers are shaped like the head of a wine glass, and are about 6 mm long. Its leaves are fairly insignificant, being tiny and narrow.

J	F	M	A	M	J	J	A	S	O	N	D

J	F	M	A	M	J	J	A	S	O	N	D

Thrift

Armeria maritima

A classic flower of the Cornish coast, thrift is found on rocky ground, among grassland and on hedgebanks all around the county. Its small, pink flowers occur tightly packed in rounded heads which are about 3 cm across. Its leaves are narrow and grass-like, but slightly fleshy. Thrift often grows in great abundance. (ES, SD)

Rock Sea-lavender

Limonium binervosum

Rock sea-lavender is a short plant, with thin but stiff flower stalks which grow to about 30 cm. The flowers are small, but attractively coloured in purple. Its leaves are oval, sometimes pointed. It grows on rocks by the sea.

Common Dodder
Cuscuta epithymum
Common dodder is an unusual plant which is parasitic, most frequently on gorse, and which climbs over its host creating a net-like appearance. Its flowers are small and pink, even clusters of these flowers are insignificant in size and can easily be overlooked. Its stem is thin but can be quite colourful, being yellow, purple or red. (ES, SD)

Betony
Stachys officinalis
Betony is quite an obvious plant which grows among long grass and on hedgebanks. Its purple flowers grow in a cylindrical spike, making a large splash of colour. Its leaves are not obvious in summer because they occur in a basal rosette. Its stem is hairy and square-sided.

J	F	M	A	M	J	J	A	S	O	N	D

J	F	M	A	M	J	J	A	S	O	N	D

Wild Thyme
Thymus praecox
Wild thyme is a mat-forming plant growing on rocky coasts and sand dunes. Its tiny flowers are pink, and can colour whole headlands. Its leaves are about ½ cm long, and are spear-shaped; they are pleasantly aromatic when crushed. (SD)

Lousewort
Pedicularis sylvatica
Lousewort is a semi-parasitic plant, taking some of its nutrients from surrounding plants. Its flowers are pink; they have a large upper lip and a three-toothed lower lip, which make a flower about 2 cm long. Lousewort grows close to the ground, often in among the short grasses and heather on acidic, damp soils.

| J | F | M | A | M | J | J | A | S | O | N | D |

| J | F | M | A | M | J | J | A | S | O | N | D |

Oxeye Daisy

Leucanthemum vulgare

This species can commonly be found by roadsides, but the plants in such places are generally cultivated: to see a genuine oxeye daisy it is best to head for the coast. It is a large-headed daisy (flowers about 30–40 cm across), with yellow disc surrounded by narrow white petals. It grows taller where cultivated, but along the coast is restricted to a height of about 30 cm.

Thyme Broomrape

Orobanche alba

Broomrapes are a group of plants that are parasitic, containing no chlorophyll. They each have a specific host plant from which they take nutrients. The thyme broomrape lives on the stems and roots of wild thyme. This species is red, and has flowers which grow on a thick stem in a spike. Each flower is like a two-lipped tube. The coastal path above Kynance Cove is a good place to see it.

| J | F | M | A | M | J | J | A | S | O | N | D |

| J | F | M | A | M | J | J | A | S | O | N | D |

Sheep's bit scabious

Jasione montana

Sometimes known simply as 'sheep's-bit', this species grows on rocky areas of coast and among grasses on hedgebanks. It rarely reaches any great height, typically 10 to 20 cm tall. Its blue flowers occur in hemispherical heads which are 2 or 3 cm across.

Bluebell

Hyacinthoides non-scripta

Often associated only with woodland, the bluebell grows very well on the Cornish coast. The violet-blue flowers hang from one side of a tall, slightly nodding stem. Its leaves are long, narrow, and slightly fleshy. A non-native variant, the Spanish bluebell, is threatening the purity of the native plant. This invasive garden escape has a stouter stem and paler blue flowers around a central stem.

| J | F | M | A | M | J | J | A | S | O | N | D |

| J | F | M | A | M | J | J | A | S | O | N | D |

Spring squill

Scilla verna

A short plant, mostly no greater than 10 cm tall, spring squill often grows in great abundance around the coast in short grassland. Its flowers are bluish-violet, a little paler than a bluebell, and grow in a domed cluster about 2 cm across. Its leaves are grass-like but fleshy, and often curled.

Montbretia

Tritonia crocosmiflora

A garden escape which has colonized freely around the Cornish coast. The tall, pale green leaves are grass-shaped, and almost as distinctive as the bright orange flowers. It can grow to about 1m tall, and its runners help it to form dense patches where little else can grow.

| J | F | M | A | M | J | J | A | S | O | N | D |

| J | F | M | A | M | J | J | A | S | O | N | D |

Green-winged Orchid
Orchis morio

A rare plant found in only a few locations. Its flowers are purple with white on the central lower lip, but it is the green veins on the upper hood (actually sepals) which give the species its name. The leaves are spear-shaped and unblotched. This orchid grows on grassland, where the soil is shallow and rocks protrude; a good area is south of Mullion around the coast path.

Heath Spotted Orchid
Dactylorhiza maculata

The heath spotted orchid is a fairly common species of orchid growing on coastal heath. Its stout stems can reach 40 cm in sheltered places, but are often stunted on the coast. The white flowers, which occur in typical orchid-shaped spikes, are patterned with pink spots. The leaves are usually marked with dark blotches.

J	F	M	A	M	J	J	A	S	O	N	D

J	F	M	A	M	J	J	A	S	O	N	D

Tar lichen

Verrucaria maura

Tar lichen is a thin, encrusting species of lichen which can look like dried oil on the rocks. It is found growing within the reach of the sea at high tide, since it can withstand periodic immersion in salt water. It can cover large areas.

Sea Ivory

Ramalina siliquosa

Sea ivory is a grey-green lichen with a bearded-like structure. It is quite brittle and dry to the touch. It grows up to about 3 cm long, usually above the splash zone of the sea. Photo: sea ivory among yellow scales.

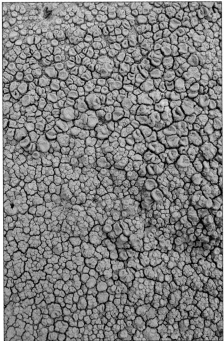

Yellow Scales
Xanthoria parietina
Yellow scales is a patch-forming lichen which is distinctive because of its bright yellow-orange colour. Patches, which grow on rocks, can be as big as 10 cm across. It grows just above the high-water mark, within the splash zone.

Crab's Eye Lichen
Ochrolechia parella
A pale grey lichen forming an encrusting patch on walls and rocks, often near the sea. The spore-producing bodies can be raised, giving a vague resemblance to crab's eyes! (CH)

Places Good for Coastal Wildlife

Place are listed alphabetically, with grid reference, location, habitat and special wildlife seen there, and notes.
Note:
- CCC – Cornwall County Council
- CWT – Cornwall Wildlife Trust
- FE – Forest Enterprise
- IOS – Isles of Scilly
- IOSWT – Isles of Scilly Wildlife Trust
- NE – Natural England
- NT – National Trust
- RSPB – Royal Society for the Protection of Birds
- SWLT – South West Lakes Trust

Bedruthan Steps, SW 84 69, Newquay. Rocky coast. Great for spring flowers

Boscastle, SX 09 91. Cliffs. Guillemot, razorbill, fulmar and spring flowers

Camel Estuary, SW 93 74, Wadebridge. Estuary. Waders and wildfowl

Cape Cornwall, SW 352 317, St Just. Headland and rock pools. Migrating seabirds

Cargreen, SX 43 62, Saltash. Estuary. Waders, particularly avocet, and wildfowl. RSPB reserve

Carnsew Pool, SW 55 37, Hayle. Tidal pool, tidal lake. Good for waders and wildfowl. RSPB reserve

Constantine Bay, SW 85 74, Padstow. Sand dunes.

Copperhouse Creek, SW 56 37, Hayle Estuary. Estuary. Wildfowl and waders. RSPB reserve

Crackington Haven, SX 14 96, Boscastle. Rock pools

Gannel Estuary, SW 79 61, Newquay. Estuary. Saltmarsh plants, wildfowl and waders

Godrevy, SW 582 432, Hayle. Headland and rock pools. Migrants, sea birds, rock pools, seals and occasional dolphins. NT

Gwithian Towans, SW 57 40, Hayle. Sand dunes. Spring flowers, butterflies, coastal grazing

Hannafore Point, SX 25 52, Looe. Rock pools

Hayle Estuary, SW 55 37, Hayle. Estuary. Saltmarsh,

waders and wildfowl. RSPB reserve

Helford, SW 75 26, Helston. Creek. Waders. Voluntary Marine Conservation Area

Jubilee Pool, SW 477 299, Penzance. Rocky coast. Purple sandpiper

Kennack Sands, SW 73 16, the Lizard. Sand dune, rock pool. Basking shark

Kynance Cove, SW 68 13, the Lizard. Rocky coast. Spring flowers, including bloody cranesbill, thyme and broomrape; coastal grazing

Lizard Point, SW 69 11, the Lizard. Headland. Migrants, sea birds and choughs; area inundated by hottentot fig

Loe Bar, SW 64 24, Helston. Barrier beach. Shingle, flowers. NT

Millpool, SX 250 538, Looe. Estuary. Waders and wildfowl

Polridmouth, SX 10 50, Fowey. Rock pools

Predannack Cliffs, SW 66 16, Mullion. Coastal heath. Green-winged orchid, other spring flowers, coastal grazing

Newlyn, SW 46 28, Newlyn. Harbour. Gulls

Nanjulian Cliffs, SW358 287, Sennen. Coastal heath. Heather, bell heather and western gorse

Padstow, SW 92 74, Padstow. Harbour and estuary. Waders (turnstones around harbour)

Pendeen Watch, SW 378 359, St Just. Headland. Sea birds

Penhale Dunes, SW 77 56, Perranporth. Dunes. Flowers and butterflies

Polly Joke, SW 77 60, Bay. Flowers, including cowslips

Polzeath, SW 936 789, Polzeath. Rock pools. Voluntary Marine Conservation Area

Porthcurno, SW 387 222, Land's End. Beach. Basking sharks

Porthgwarra, SW 371 218, St Just. Headland. Seabirds and migrants

Rame Head, SX 41 48, Torpoint. Headland. Birds such as peregrine and raven, coastal grazing

Ruan Lanihorne, SW 88 41, Tregony. Estuary. Salt marsh plants and waders

St Agnes Head, SW 698 515, St Agnes. Heathland. Heathers and western gorse

St Ives, SW 51 40. Harbour. Turnstones, sea birds

St John's Lake, SX 42 54, Torpoint. Estuary. Waders and wildfowl

The Mouls, SW 93 81, Wadebridge. Island. Puffins

Upton Towans, SW 57 39, Hayle. Dunes. Flowers and butterflies. CWT reserve

Wacker Quay, SX 389 551, Torpoint. Estuary. Wildfowl and waders

Index

Organizations and Groups

Cornwall Birds (previously The Cornwall
Bird-Watching & Preservation Society)
Membership secretary: Sara McMahon
Tel: 01752 242 823
Email: sara@surfbirder.com

**Cornwall County Council,
Environment & Heritage Section**
Cornwall County Council, Old County Hall,
Truro TR1 3AY
Tel: 01872 222 000
www.cornwall.gov.uk

Cornwall Wildlife Trust
Five Acres, Allet, nr Truro TR4 9DJ
Tel: 01872 273 939
www.cornwallwildlifetrust.org.uk

Helford Voluntary Marine Conservation Area
(HVMCA)
Co-ordinator: Dr Pamela Tompsett
c/o Cornwall Wildlife Trust
www.helfordmarineconservation.co.uk

Isles of Scilly Wildlife Trust
Carn Thomas, St Mary's,
Isles of Scilly TR21 0PT
Tel: 01720 422 153
www.ios-wildlife-trust.org.uk

National Trust, Cornwall Office
Lanhydrock, Bodmin PL30 4DE
Tel: 01208 742 81
www.nationaltrust.org.uk

**Natural England,
Cornwall & Isles of Scilly Team**
Trevint House, Strangways Villas,
Truro TR1 2PA
Tel: 01872 265 710,
head office 01733 455 000
www.naturalengland.org.uk

**North Cornwall District Council,
Coast & Countryside Service**
3/5 Barn Lane, Bodmin PL31 1LZ
Tel: 01208 863181
www.ncdc.gov.uk

Royal Society for the Protection of Birds
The RSPB South West Regional Office,
Keble House, Southernhay Gardens,
Exeter EX1 1NT
Tel: 01392 432 691
www.rspb.org.uk